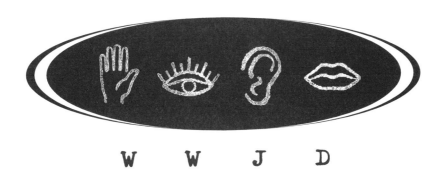

W   W   J   D

Spiritual Challenge
Journal

More student journals for you from Youth Specialties!

Grow For It Journal

Grow For It Journal through the Scriptures

Wild Truth Journal for Junior Highers

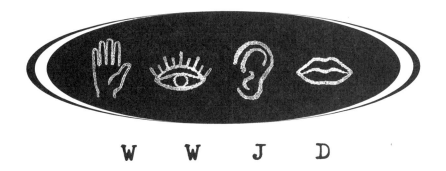

W W J D

Spiritual Challenge
Journal

A 30-day faith-in-action adventure
for students

Mike Yaconelli

ZondervanPublishingHouse

Grand Rapids, Michigan
A Division of HarperCollinsPublishers

Edited by Tim McLaughlin (He raises rabbits, for crying out loud.)
Interior design by Patton Brothers Design (They're not really brothers.)

Printed in the United States of America (O say can you see?)

c o n t e n t s

Intro
Would this be cool or what? You open the door to head for school, and there he is—Jesus.

Prep
For the next 30 days you are going to ask yourself, *What would Jesus do?* in every circumstance of your life.

Pre
What are your expectations for the next 30 days?

The 30-day adventure

Mid

How are you doing now, considering the expectations you wrote down at the beginning?

Post

A letter to Jesus.

Would this be cool or what? You open the door to head for school, and there he is—Jesus. You know it's him because . . . well, you just know. Hey, you're gonna *know* when Jesus shows up. But we're not talking about the end of the world here. We're talking about Jesus standing in your front yard, ready to go to school with you.

Cool, right?

It's not like he's not spooky or anything. He doesn't look weird like the pictures in your Bible, but it's still kinda strange to see him in your front yard. The question you've gotta answer is this: Are you gonna trash the whole day, or are you and Jesus going to school—*together*?

Talk about a trip. Imagine the conversation with your friends in the hall before first period:

"Hey, what's happening, guys? . . . Huh? Oh, this guy? He's cool. His name is Jesus. . . seriously, I'm not kidding. . . no, not *like* that guy in the Bible—he *is* that guy from the Bible. This is the *real* Jes—hey, where are you going?"

Okay, so maybe you're not all that excited about taking Jesus to school. To be honest, Jesus could screw up your day, big time. Think about it—Jesus and you in class, at lunch in the quad, in the locker room, at football practice. Yeah, well, football practice might be a kick. What would the coach say with Jesus standing there? Could be a very quiet practice.

How about after school—**Jesus with you and your girlfriend?** Whoa. That could be a disaster for your love life. Not a whole lot you can do with Jesus sitting in the car.

Jesus with you at home—what would that be like? You couldn't argue with your folks. You'd have to treat your sister decently. You'd probably have to turn the stereo down. You might even have to turn it off. I mean, what kind of music does Jesus listen to? Oh man, what if it's *country*?

Face it: having Jesus hang around you all day could have a seriously weird effect on your life.

Can you imagine walking around all the time thinking about what Jesus would do? Man, talk about instant nomination for Nerd of the Year.

Having Jesus around all the time could ruin your life—in a way you might not expect. It might ruin your life in a *good* way. The idea may seem strange, **but maybe your life needs to be ruined by**

Jesus. Imagine Jesus "ruining" your life by causing every day to be a wild, mysterious adventure filled with risk and surprise. Having Jesus around might even be fun—the kind of deep-down-inside fun that comes from knowing you and Jesus are buds, friends. Imagine the fun of seeing the smile of Jesus—the kind of smile that says, "I know you tried to do what I would do. You screwed up a few times, but you're still cool because you're trying. I know I'm not easy to follow. Even my disciples couldn't figure out where I was going or what I was doing."

Okay, maybe you don't see Jesus standing in your front yard right now, but what if he was? What if he *is?* His body may not be there, but what if the Bible really is true when it says that Jesus is with us. Now. Right here. You can't see him with your eyes, but if you think about it, maybe you can see him in your mind. Maybe you could see him in your heart if every day you asked yourself over and over, *What would Jesus do?* All day long just keep thinking, *What would Jesus do?* What if this simple question could keep Jesus present in your mind and invite him into every part of your life?

Hmmm.

What would happen if day-after-day for an entire month you kept asking yourself, *What would Jesus do?* Why, you might find yourself **actually trying to live** a life Jesus would have lived. And, maybe, if you staring living like Jesus, you might find someone saying to you, "Hey, are you Jesus?" Okay, that probably wouldn't happen.

Or would it?

Nobody could mistake you for Jesus, could they? Could they?

Are you freaked out yet? Ready to take a chance? Ready to risk a month of your life? Ready to have the next 30 days "ruined" by Jesus? Ready to participate in a 30-day adventure with Jesus? Ready to blow yourself and your friends away by bringing Jesus with you wherever you go? Ready to have the best 30 days of your life?

Fasten your seat belt, **put on your crash helmet,** hang on with every bit of strength you have, and let the adventure begin.

For the next 30 days you are going to ask yourself, What would Jesus do? in every circumstance of your life. No one will know except you. Based on what you know of

Jesus and what you're going to learn about him in these next 30 days, you're going to try to do what you think Jesus would do.

Before you begin, here are some questions you'll probably want answered.

How do I know what Jesus would do?

You don't. Hey, no big deal. Neither did any other people when they were with Jesus. Remember the disciples? The guys who tried to keep the little kids from Jesus? The guys who told Jesus not to die? The guys who got angry when Jesus had expensive perfume poured over him? They weren't exactly scholars in Jesusology.

Let's get this straight. Nobody knows for sure what Jesus would do in any situation. But when you read about him in the New Testament, you can recognize some clues.

Clue: Jesus always did the unexpected.

Jesus touched lepers when everyone else ran from them. He hung out with people he wasn't supposed to be around—traitors, children, prostitutes, and Samaritans. He didn't act religious—in fact, he made the religious leaders mad. He wasn't politically correct.

He wasn't any-kind-of correct. The people around him said winning was everything. He said if you want to win, you have to lose. "Live as long as you can!" they shouted. He laughed and said, "If you want life, you have to die." Most every time Jesus spoke, the crowds responded with a resounding "Huh?"

When you ask the question "What would Jesus do?" think about the unexpectedness of his responses. Remember, Jesus doesn't think like everyone else thinks. Let your thinking run wild—just like his.

Clue: Whatever Jesus did, he upset people.

Asking what Jesus would do could be hazardous to your friendships, your dating life, and your relationship with your parents. Jesus kept telling his disciples, "Follow me and it could cost you everything." If you follow Jesus' example, don't expect everyone to flock around you and want to be your friend. Jesus had good friends and plenty of enemies. Try to do what Jesus would do, and you'll find out who your friends are. You might even make some new ones. Of course, you might make some new enemies, too. That's the adventure part.

✋ Clue: When Jesus did something, it was costly.

Doing what Jesus did isn't easy. Jesus and his followers had no place to live, no money. Toward the end of their journey together their lives were in danger. They gave up their families, their careers, their security. Many people considered the followers of Christ—that is, those who wanted to do what Jesus did—to be crazy, drunk, or both. It's costly to follow Christ. Do what he did, and you might find yourself wondering if following Jesus is worth it. Trust us (and trust him)—it's worth it.

✋ Clue: When Jesus did something, people's lives were changed.

The woman caught in adultery, blind Bartimaeus, the lepers, the woman with the blood disease, the little girl who was dying—Jesus left changed lives wherever he went. If you try to do what Jesus would do, one thing is for sure: lives will be changed, and changed for the better. That doesn't mean you're going to see people changing right in front of your eyes. Sometimes you just have to trust that they're changing. Trust the truth. Trust Jesus. Whether you can see any results or not, following Jesus always results in changed lives.

✋ Clue: Jesus spent a lot of time doing nothing, which was actually something.

This is very important. What Jesus *did* resulted from who Jesus *was.* His doing was directly connected to his being. He was constantly getting away from the crowds to be with his Father. Jesus knew intimacy was more important than activity. During your 30-day adventure, you'll find that one clear answer to the question *What would Jesus do?* is—nothing. He would spend time alone, silent, praying, being with his Father, waiting. Don't think of this adventure as some*thing* you have to do all the time, but as some*one* Christ is calling you to be.

✋ Clue: Jesus failed—at least it looked that way.

We know now that Jesus didn't fail, but it sure looked like failure two thousand years ago. Of course, it didn't take long for some of his followers to figure out that he hadn't failed. In fact, most of them ended up losing their lives for Jesus' sake—and they seemed happy to do so. So what's the deal? Simple. Do what Jesus did and you will live a life that is full, exciting, and—well, dangerous. Do what Jesus did and you may discover that the world—including friends and family members—thinks you're a failure. Jesus, though, will be smiling because he's been there, done that. Following Jesus isn't about success, it's about faithfulness. Following Jesus may result in suffering, pain, or even death. What you will discover is that Jesus is present even in our suffering, even in our pain. Jesus didn't promise we would all be winners—he said winning didn't matter because, in the kingdom of God, even losers win.

Do I tell people what I'm doing?

No. This 30-day adventure is between you and Jesus. It's a little secret that has everything to do with your relationship to Jesus, not your relationship with others.
Remember how many times Jesus said to his disciples, "Don't tell anyone about me.
Don't tell them what you've seen"? Wonder why he did that? When Mary was pregnant with Jesus, Luke tells us "she kept these things and pondered them in her heart."
She didn't tell anyone. There is something about keeping secrets that is important. Let
this adventure be a secret between you and Jesus.

But what if a bunch of my friends are doing this adventure, too?

Cool. Just don't make yourselves obvious. No public meetings on campus. No group
prayers in front of everyone. Just meet privately and pray for each other. Remember, it's
important to keep this a secret between you and Jesus. Wear your WWJD bracelet, of
course, and respond to kid's questions about what the letters mean, but don't make them
think they're part of an experiment or something. Remember, though, you don't want to
keep *Jesus* a secret—just your 30-day adventure. Meet with your group, share your journals
and your experiences, but make sure your daily experience is just between you and Jesus.

What is my goal—to make all my friends Christians?

Sure, ultimately—but our goal is a goal within a goal. Our goal is to pay attention to the
presence of Jesus in our lives with the hope that those around us will get a glimpse of
Jesus. We already know what will happen when people see Jesus. They will either fall on
their knees or run for cover. Falling on their knees may take a long time—their glimpse of
Jesus may be the beginning of a three-year falling or a ten-year falling. Regardless, they
will have begun their journey with Jesus because of his presence in your life.

Constantly praying "What would Jesus do?" seems artificial and phony. What am I sup-posed to do, act like some kind of saint?

The worst thing you can do is act like a perfect person. Jesus was around such sup-
posedly perfect people all the time and he didn't think much of them (read Matthew
25). Don't try to act like the Jesus in the movies. Just be yourself. Do what you always
do, only let the question *What would Jesus do?* soak into your brain and into your
soul. Then just see what happens. You will probably be as surprised as the next person. You may find yourself having lunch with a loner at school who has been rejected
by everyone—not because it's something you're supposed to do, but because you're
suddenly drawn to that person. Don't pretend, don't calculate. Just let the presence of
Jesus in you surprise you.

pre

The beginning of my 30-day adventure

Write down all of your expectations for the next 30 days. Include your expectations for your relationship with Jesus, your parents, your friends, your school, your job, and your church. What do you want to see happen in the next 30 days?

My expectation for the next 30 days as I think of—

My relationship with Jesus...

My parents...

My friends...

My school...

My job...

My church and youth group...

And other important stuff in my life now...

Parent **problems**

Seems like every day I'm getting hassled by my parents. We fight all the time. If it's not my room, it's my homework, my music, my clothes, my friends, my choices. I guess there are good moments, but not very many and not very often. I don't get it. I'm not saying it's all their fault, I'm just saying I thought Jesus would make my family better. When I get into arguments with my family, I try to stop myself, but it never works. I always end up saying something I wish I hadn't said. My parents are always criticizing me. I never hear anything positive or good about what I'm doing. Course, I don't talk to them much anymore either. How can I make my family better?

What do you think Jesus would do?

Jesus and his parents *Luke 2:41-52*

Every year his parents went to Jerusalem for the Feast of the Passover. When he was 12 years old, they went up to the Feast, according to the custom. After the Feast was over, while his parents were returning home, the boy Jesus stayed behind in Jerusalem, but they were unaware of it. Thinking he was in their company, they traveled on for a day. Then they began looking for him among their relatives and friends. When they did not find him, they went back to Jerusalem to look for him. After three days they found him in the temple courts, sitting among the teachers, listening to them and asking them questions. Everyone who heard him was amazed at his understanding and his answers. When his parents saw him, they were astonished. His mother said to him, "Son, why have you treated us like this? Your father and I have been anxiously searching for you."

"Why were you searching for me?" he asked. "Didn't you know I had to be in my Father's house?" But they did not understand what he was saying to them.

Then he went down to Nazareth with them and was obedient to them. But his mother treasured all these things in her heart. And Jesus grew in wisdom and stature, and in favor with God and men.

What did Jesus do?

According to verse 51 Jesus went home and "was obedient" to his parents after he ditched them for three days. They were very upset. What do you think of Jesus' answer to his parents? Is obeying your parents a non-negotiable, or are there some exceptions?

Real-life response

Look for someone who appears to be really hurting. It doesn't matter whether or not you know the person's name. Pray for him. If there's anything you feel you can do for the person, do it.

So how'd it go today?

1. Were you conscious of Jesus at all today? If so, when? If not, why not?

2. What, if anything, did you notice about yourself today?

3. What do you want to say to Jesus after today?
> Dear Jesus,

4. What would Jesus say to you after today?
> Dear _____,

day 2

Mark and the locker gorillas

Mark recognized the two guys standing at his locker. The day before he had seen them cut some locks and steal two mountain bikes from the school bike rack. Apparently they had seen him. They looked like gorillas standing at his locker.

Great, Mark thought. Now I'm gonna get my face ripped off.

The two boys made it very clear that if Mark said anything to anyone, he wouldn't like the consequences. It wasn't a difficult decision. Mark decided to keep his mouth shut.

What do you think Jesus would do?

Jesus and the wild animals *Mark 1:12-13; Matthew 4:1-11*

At once the Spirit sent him out into the desert, and he was in the desert forty days, being tempted by Satan. He was with the wild animals, and angels attended him.

Then Jesus was led by the Spirit into the desert to be tempted by the devil. After fasting forty days and forty nights, he was hungry. The tempter came to him and said, "If you are the Son of God, tell these stones to become bread."

Jesus answered, "It is written: 'Man does not live on bread alone, but on every word that comes from the mouth of God.' "

Then the devil took him to the holy city and had him stand on the highest point of the temple. "If you are the son of God," he said, "throw yourself down. For it is written: 'He will command his angels concerning you, and they will lift you up in their hands, so that you will not strike your foot against a stone.' "

Jesus answered him, "It is also written: 'Do not put the Lord your God to the test.' "

Again, the devil took him to a very high mountain and showed him all the kingdoms of the world and their splendor. "All this I will give you," he said, "if you will bow down and worship me."

Jesus said to him, "Away from me, Satan! For it is written: 'Worship the Lord your God, and serve him only.' "

Then the devil left him, and the angels came and attended him.

What did Jesus do?
Jesus resisted the way of power, popularity, and wealth. Can you think of any situations in your life right now where you're being asked to resist these things?

Real-life response

Think of someone at school who is always criticizing or making fun of Christianity. Try to say a prayer for that person every time the bell rings today.

So how'd it go today?

1. Were you conscious of Jesus at all today? If so, when? If not, why not?

2. What, if anything, did you notice about yourself today?

3. What do you want to say to Jesus after today?
    Dear Jesus,

4. What would Jesus say to you after today?

    Dear _____ ,

day 3

Cara and the rain man

As long as Cara can remember—as far back as second grade, when they first met—she's felt sorry for her friend Howard because he's always been the butt of jokes. They've had a long friendship, and Howard has always been a part of Cara's life. Cara has become very attractive as a high schooler, and although she has many admirers, her friendship with Howard has never been in question. Until now. Now Howard seems possessive and jealous. In fact, two nights ago he called and asked Cara to go out with him. Cara was shocked. Go out with Howard? Not a chance. Howard as a friend, fine—but Howard as a boyfriend, never. Howard was nowhere near good looking—and he was overweight, too. On the other hand, Cara thought, he was a sad person who could really use a friend. Now what? Say no and wreck their friendship? Or say yes and wreck their friendship?

What do you think Jesus would do?

Jesus and the strange man *Mark 1:40-45*

A man with leprosy came to him and begged him on his knees, "If you are willing, you can make me clean."

Filled with compassion, Jesus reached out his hand and touched the man. "I am willing," he said. "Be clean!" Immediately the leprosy left him and he was cured.

Jesus sent him away at once with a strong warning: "See that you don't tell this to anyone. But go, show yourself to the priest and offer the sacrifices that Moses command-ed for your cleansing, as a testimony to them." Instead he went out and began to talk freely, spreading the news. As a result, Jesus could no longer enter a town openly but stayed outside in lonely places. Yet the people still came to him from everywhere.

What did Jesus do?
Jesus told the leper not to tell anyone what had happened. The leper did anyway. If you were the leper, what would you have done? Why?

Real-life response

Think of a "leper" in your school, someone who's avoided by most everyone. Find a way to anonymously affirm that person today.

So **how'd it** go today?

1. Were you conscious of Jesus at all today? If so, when? If not, why not?

2. What, if anything, did you notice about yourself today?

3. What do you want to say to Jesus after today?
    Dear Jesus,

4. What would Jesus say to you after today?
    Dear _____ ,

day 4

Fear at school

I don't want to go to school today. The racial tensions are so thick you can cut them with a knife. Speaking of knives, who knows how many kids have weapons on campus? There are fights almost every day and rumors of fights all the time. Violence isn't some rare occurrence happening to other people, it's here on this campus right now. A lot of my friends are attending private schools. I don't know what to do. My parents can't afford to send me to a private school, and I'm not sure I'd go anyway. All I know is I'm scared all the time. I don't know what to do.

What do you think Jesus would do?

Fear at home (hometown boy does bad) *Luke 4:14-30*

Jesus returned to Galilee in the power of the Spirit, and news about him spread through the whole countryside. He taught in their synagogues, and everyone praised him.

He went to Nazareth, where he had been brought up, and on the Sabbath day he went into the synagogue, as was his custom. And he stood up to read. The scroll of the prophet Isaiah was handed to him. Unrolling it, he found the place where it is written: "The Spirit of the Lord is on me, because he has anointed me to preach good news to the poor. He has sent me to proclaim freedom for the prisoners and recovery of sight for the blind, to release the oppressed, to proclaim the year of the Lord's favor."

Then he rolled up the scroll, gave it back to the attendant and sat down. The eyes of everyone in the synagogue were fastened on him, and he began by saying to them, "Today this scripture is fulfilled in your hearing."

All spoke well of him and were amazed at the gracious words that came from his lips. "Isn't this Joseph's son?" they asked.

Jesus said to them, "Surely you will quote this proverb to me: 'Physician, heal yourself! Do here in your hometown what we have heard that you did in Capernaum.' "

"I tell you the truth," he continued, "no prophet is accepted in his hometown. I assure you that there were many widows in Israel in Elijah's time, when the sky was shut for three and a half years and there was a severe famine throughout the land. Yet Elijah was not sent to any of them, but to a widow in Zarephath in the region of Sidon. And there were many in Israel with leprosy in the time of Elisha the prophet, yet not one of them was cleansed—only Naaman the Syrian."

All the people in the synagogue were furious when they heard this. They got up,

drove him out of the town, and took him to the brow of the hill on which the town was built, in order to throw him down the cliff. But he walked right through the crowd and went on his way.

What did Jesus do?
You're saying something about Jesus when suddenly the person you're talking to replies, "Oh, excuse me, Mother Teresa. I didn't know you were a saint. I thought you were my next-door neighbor, the one who used to sneak out with me late at night for a smoke." What would you say?

Real-life response

What do you fear most at school? List a few practical ways to overcome your fear. Try one or more of your ideas today to see if it works.

So how'd it go today?

1. Were you conscious of Jesus at all today? If so, when? If not, why not?

2. What, if anything, did you notice about yourself today?

3. What do you want to say to Jesus after today?
　　　Dear Jesus,

4. What would Jesus say to you after today?
　　　Dear _____,

day 5

No place to go

Denise's home life is horrible, and it's getting worse. She hates her stepfather. Actually, she's afraid of him. More than once he has made sexual advances toward her. Denise is afraid to tell anyone about her fears. Her mother believes God led her to this man, so Denise doubts her mother would believe her. The first divorce was so ugly and painful, Denise couldn't bear putting her mother through another one. Besides, in only one more year Denise will be out of the house.

Sometimes Denise wonders if the situation is partly her fault. She was pretty affectionate with her stepdad at first because her real father had been an alcoholic and so distant. Denise has told no one about the situation, not even her boyfriend. She doesn't know what to do.

What do you think Jesus would do?

Only one place to go   *John 6:60-69*

On hearing it, many of his disciples said, "This is a hard teaching. Who can accept it?"

Aware that his disciples were grumbling about this, Jesus said to them, "Does this offend you? What if you see the Son of Man ascend to where he was before! The Spirit gives life; the flesh counts for nothing. The words I have spoken to you are spirit and they are life. Yet there are some of you who do not believe." For Jesus had known from the beginning which of them did not believe and who would betray him. He went on to say, "This is why I told you that no one can come to me unless the Father has enabled him."

From this time many of his disciples turned back and no longer followed him. "You do not want to leave too, do you?" Jesus asked the Twelve.

Simon Peter answered him, "Lord, to whom shall we go? You have the words of eternal life. We believe and know that you are the Holy One of God."

What did Peter say?
If Jesus asked the same question to you, what would your honest response be?

Real-life response

Repeat to yourself all day long the phrase, "Lord, who else would I go to besides you?"

So **how'd it** go today?

**1. Were you conscious of Jesus at all today? If so, when?
If not, why not?**

2. What, if anything, did you notice about yourself today?

3. What do you want to say to Jesus after today?
    Dear Jesus,

4. What would Jesus say to you after today?
    Dear _____,

day 6

Over her head

Cherie was one of the girls. She had been best friends with four other girls since junior high school, and now they're all seniors. They all went to the same church, the same Young Life Club, the same parties. They took care of each other and held each other accountable when it looked like one of them was stuck in the deep end.

But something happened this past summer. Cherie went on a mission trip and a family vacation and was gone most of the summer. When she returned she couldn't believe her girlfriends were the same people. All of them were into the party scene—drinking, getting physical with guys, smoking. At first Cherie tried fitting in, but she just couldn't. Now she's being forced to do something. All her friends talked to her after school and told her she was no fun anymore. They said it was fine if she wanted to be a dweeb, but they didn't want her keeping them from having a good time. They told her to knock off all the God stuff and just be a friend. The implication was clear: If you don't knock off the God stuff, you'll have no friends anymore.

As you can imagine, Cherie is pretty depressed. How can she get through her senior year without her best friends?

What would Jesus do?

The cost of telling a lie *Matthew 26:33-35, 69-75*

Peter replied, "Even if all fall away on account of you, I never will."

"I tell you the truth," Jesus answered, "this very night, before the rooster crows, you will disown me three times."

But Peter declared, "Even if I have to die with you, I will never disown you." And all the other disciples said the same. . . .

Now Peter was sitting out in the courtyard, and a servant girl came to him. "You also were with Jesus of Galilee," she said.

But he denied it before them all. "I don't know what you're talking about," he said.

Then he went out to the gateway, where another girl saw him and said to the people there, "This fellow was with Jesus of Nazareth."

He denied it again, with an oath: "I don't know the man!"

After a little while, those standing there went up to Peter and said, "Surely you are one of them, for your accent gives you away."

Then he began to call down curses on himself and he swore to them, "I don't know the man!"

Immediately a rooster crowed. Then Peter remembered the word Jesus had spoken: "Before the rooster crows, you will disown me three times." And he went outside and wept bitterly.

What did Jesus do?

Peter denied strongly that he would betray Christ, but he did. Why do you believe Peter was so clueless about himself? Do you see any warning for you in this story?

Real-life response

Think of someone who has betrayed you. If you haven't forgiven that person yet, write his first name down in a place where you'll see it often. Every time you see the person's name, pray for him.

So how'd it go today?

1. Were you conscious of Jesus at all today? If so, when? If not, why not?

2. What, if anything, did you notice about yourself today?

3. What do you want to say to Jesus after today?
   Dear Jesus,

4. What would Jesus say to you after today?
Dear _____ ,

day 7

When life gets dark

The week started off bad and got worse. Dad was laid off on Monday. Mom hasn't worked in two months because of a bad back. My brother, Daniel, has something weird wrong with him that the doctors can't figure out. They just keep saying they don't think it's cancer. I've been trying to cover for mom around the house and spend time with Dan. That's why my grades are hurting pretty badly. I'm really trying, but I'm just so burnt out. Where the heck is Jesus, anyway? I prayed like crazy that Dad wouldn't lose his job. A lot of good it did, too.

What do you think Jesus would do?

Life got dark for him, too *Matthew 26:36-46*

Then Jesus went with his disciples to a place called Gethsemane, and he said to them, "Sit here while I go over there and pray." He took Peter and the two sons of Zebedee along with him, and he began to be sorrowful and troubled. Then he said to them, "My soul is overwhelmed with sorrow to the point of death. Stay here and keep watch with me."

Going a little farther, he fell with his face to the ground and prayed, "My Father, if it is possible, may this cup be taken from me. Yet not as I will, but as you will." Then he returned to his disciples and found them sleeping. "Could you men not keep watch with me for one hour?" he asked Peter. "Watch and pray so that you will not fall into temptation. The spirit is willing, but the body is weak."

He went away a second time and prayed, "My Father, if it is not possible for this cup to be taken away unless I drink it, may your will be done."

When he came back, he again found them sleeping, because their eyes were heavy. So he left them and went away once more and prayed the third time, saying the same thing.

Then he returned to the disciples and said to them, "Are you still sleeping and resting? Look, the hour is near, and the Son of Man is betrayed into the hands of sinners. Rise, let us go! Here comes my betrayer!"

What did Jesus do?

Jesus hoped he could escape the cross by praying. He couldn't. What does this incident teach you about prayer, especially in light of Jesus' statement in verse 42: "If it is not possible for this cup to be taken away unless I drink it, may your will be done"?

Real-life response

Surprise your parents this morning by cleaning up your room and straightening up around the entire house before you leave.

So how'd it go today?

1. Were you conscious of Jesus at all today? If so, when? If not, why not?

2. What, if anything, did you notice about yourself today?

3. What do you want to say to Jesus after today?
    Dear Jesus,

4. What would Jesus say to you after today?
    Dear _____,

No big deal

Sue is telling another gross joke. Every time the girls get together, Sue has a dirty joke to tell. Jennifer has no idea where Sue gets these jokes. . .but they *are* pretty funny. Jennifer's youth director says Christians shouldn't listen to crude jokes. Maybe so, but it's not that easy. Everyone tells them. What are you supposed to do, plug your ears? Jennifer thinks as long as she doesn't repeat the jokes, there's no harm done. She says the only way to avoid hearing crude jokes is to become a hermit.

What do you believe Jesus would do in Jennifer's situation?

Big deal *John 2:13-22*

When it was almost time for the Jewish Passover, Jesus went up to Jerusalem. In the temple courts he found men selling cattle, sheep and doves, and others sitting at tables exchanging money. So he made a whip out of cords, and drove all from the temple area, both sheep and cattle; he scattered the coins of the money changers and overturned their tables. To those who sold doves he said, "Get these out of here! How dare you turn my Father's house into a market!"

His disciples remembered that it is written: "Zeal for your house will consume me."

Then the Jews demanded of him, "What miraculous sign can you show us to prove your authority to do all this?"

Jesus answered them, "Destroy this temple, and I will raise it again in three days." The Jews replied, "It has taken forty-six years to build this temple, and you are going to raise it in three days?" But the temple he had spoken of was his body. After he was raised from the dead, his disciples recalled what he had said. Then they believed the Scripture and the words that Jesus had spoken.

What did Jesus do?
Jesus was angry that the very people who were supposed to defend the holiness of God were actually diminishing the holiness of God. In other words, those who use the name of Christ should be careful how they portray Christ in their lives. What should Christians do when they hear the name of Christ being diminished?

Real-life response

Write your brother, sister, or best friend a letter of affirmation, telling that person how much you appreciate who he is.

So how'd it go today?

1. Were you conscious of Jesus at all today? If so, when? If not, why not?

2. What, if anything, did you notice about yourself today?

3. What do you want to say to Jesus after today?
    Dear Jesus,

4. What would Jesus say to you after today?
    Dear _____,

day 9

Degrading women

"Hi, Linda. Your sweater is sure looking good . . . uh, I mean, you're looking good . . . um, both of you."

Todd and his three buddies look at each other and start laughing hysterically. Linda likes Todd a lot, but his crude comments are starting to make her mad. She doesn't want to blow a chance to go out with him, but every time she asks him to knock it off, he says he's just kidding. Last time she told him she didn't think he was kidding.

Todd just smiled. "What are you?" he said. "Some kind of feminazi?" Linda doesn't know what to do.

What do you think Jesus would say to Todd?

A degraded woman upgraded *John 8:1-11*

But Jesus went to the Mount of Olives. At dawn he appeared again in the temple courts, where all the people gathered around him, and he sat down to teach them. The teachers of the law and the Pharisees brought in a woman caught in adultery. They made her stand before the group and said to Jesus, "Teacher, this woman was caught in the act of adultery. In the Law Moses commanded us to stone such women. Now what do you say?" They were using this question as a trap, in order to have a basis for accusing him.

But Jesus bent down and started to write on the ground with his finger. When they kept on questioning him, he straightened up and said to them, "If any one of you is without sin, let him be the first to throw a stone at her." Again he stooped down and wrote on the ground.

At this, those who heard began to go away one at a time, the older ones first, until only Jesus was left, with the woman still standing there. Jesus straightened up and asked her, "Woman, where are they? Has no one condemned you?"

"No one, sir," she said.

"Then neither do I condemn you," Jesus declared. "Go now and leave your life of sin."

What did Jesus do?
Who do you identify with most in the story? Why?

Real-life response

Look for someone who is alone at school today. Try to start a conversation with the person or maybe just sit down with him at lunch or snack break. Don't try to witness to him—just try to get him talking and listen to what he says.

So how'd it go today?

1. Were you conscious of Jesus at all today? If so, when? If not, why not?

2. What, if anything, did you notice about yourself today?

3. What do you want to say to Jesus after today?
     Dear Jesus,

4. What would Jesus say to you after today?
     Dear _____,

day 10

Put up or shut up

Kirk is making fun of Stan again. Nothing new. It's been going on since sixth grade. Stan is a senior and has a dancing part in the school play. Kirk says any guy who wears leotards is gay. To be honest, Stan doesn't know if he's gay or not. He's never been interested in dating girls, but neither is he attracted to guys. He doesn't know what he is, but he does take his Christian faith seriously. He has tried to be nice to Kirk, but Kirk doesn't understand nice.

Stan's never been in a fight before, but enough is enough. He knows he can wipe the sidewalk with Kirk, but he frankly doesn't want to fight Kirk. After today, however, what Stan wants is no longer an issue. Kirk is standing in front of him, keeping him from making rehearsal on time, and saying, "If you want me to move, faggot, you'll have to make me move."

What do you think Jesus would do if he were Stan?

Call in the big boys   *Matthew 26:47-56*

While he was still speaking, Judas, one of the Twelve, arrived. With him was a large crowd armed with swords and clubs, sent from the chief priests and the elders of the people. Now the betrayer had arranged a signal with them: "The one I kiss is the man; arrest him." Going at once to Jesus, Judas said, "Greetings, Rabbi!" and kissed him.

Jesus replied, "Friend, do what you came for."
Then the men stepped forward, seized Jesus and arrested him. With that, one of Jesus' companions reached for his sword, drew it out and struck the servant of the high priest, cutting off his ear.

"Put your sword back in its place," Jesus said to him, "for all who draw the sword will die by the sword. Do you think I cannot call on my Father, and he will at once put at my disposal more than 12 legions of angels? But how then would the Scriptures be fulfilled that say it must happen in this way?"

At that time Jesus said to the crowd, "Am I leading a rebellion, that you have come out with swords and clubs to capture me? Every day I sat in the temple courts teaching, and you did not arrest me. But this has all taken place that the writings of the prophets might be fulfilled." Then all the disciples deserted him and fled.

What did Jesus do?

Notice that Jesus called Judas "friend." What does it mean to be a friend of Jesus?

Real-life response

Be a "secret friend" and leave an anonymous gift for each of your friends today.

So how'd it go today?

1. Were you conscious of Jesus at all today? If so, when? If not, why not?

2. What, if anything, did you notice about yourself today?

3. What do you want to say to Jesus after today?
     Dear Jesus,

4. What would Jesus say to you after today?
     Dear _____,

day 11

What are friends for?

Kerry Allen has been on everyone's mind at school. He was a six-foot-seven All-State basketball champ on his way to a big college with a full-ride athletic scholarship. And then the accident happened. What a freak deal—right there in the quad in front of everyone. One of the school maintenance trucks popped out of gear and rolled into a bunch of students during break. Lots of bumps and bruises, but no one seriously hurt—except Kerry, whose spine was crushed when the truck pinned him against a wall. Now he can't feel anything in his legs.

      The accident was two months ago, but everyone's still talking about it. Mike and his friends have known Kerry for a long time. They really believe God can heal Kerry. They are ready to pray for him—you know, the kind of praying where everyone lays hands on Kerry and asks God to heal him. But what if the praying doesn't work? Will everyone make fun of the guys? Will they make fun of God? Mike and his buddies don't know what to do.

What do you think Jesus would do if he were Mike?

House wreckers *Mark 2:1-12*

A few days later, when Jesus again entered Capernaum, the people heard that he had come home. So many gathered that there was no room left, not even outside the door, and he preached the word to them. Some men came, bringing to him a paralytic, carried by four of them. Since they could not get him to Jesus because of the crowd, they made an opening in the roof above Jesus and, after digging through it, lowered the mat the paralyzed man was lying on. When Jesus saw their faith, he said to the paralytic, "Son, your sins are forgiven."

      Now some teachers of the law were sitting there, thinking to themselves, "Why does this fellow talk like that? He's blaspheming! Who can forgive sins but God alone?"

      Immediately Jesus knew in his spirit that this was what they were thinking in their hearts, and he said to them, "Why are you thinking these things? Which is easier: to say to the paralytic, 'Your sins are forgiven,' or to say, 'Get up, take your mat and walk'? But that you may know that the Son of Man has authority on earth to forgive sins. . . ." He said to the paralytic, "I tell you, get up, take your mat and go home." He got up, took his mat and walked out in full view of them all. This amazed everyone and they praised God, saying, "We have never seen anything like this!"

What did Jesus do?

The men in this story were willing to damage someone else's property to help their friend. How far would you go—or should you go—to bring a friend to Jesus?

Real-life response

Think of a friend who is not a Christian. Pray all day for an opportunity to talk to that person about your faith.

So how'd it go today?

1. Were you conscious of Jesus at all today? If so, when? If not, why not?

2. What, if anything, did you notice about yourself today?

3. What do you want to say to Jesus after today?
     Dear Jesus,

4. What would Jesus say to you after today?
     Dear _____,

No hope

There are a bunch of kids in our school who are into gangs. Mean and angry, they seem hopelessly lost in a world I know nothing about. People say that anyone can change, but I don't believe it. I really think there are kids at our school who are already beyond hope. Let's put it this way: there's no way *I* could ever get close to gangbangers. They wouldn't like me. Some of them might even want to hurt me.

What would Jesus do?

No hope? *Luke 23:39-43*

One of the criminals who hung there hurled insults at him: "Aren't you the Christ? Save yourself and us!"

But the other criminal rebuked him. "Don't you fear God," he said, "since you are under the same sentence? We are punished justly, for we are getting what our deeds deserve. But this man has done nothing wrong."

Then he said, "Jesus, remember me when you come into your kingdom."

Jesus answered him, "I tell you the truth, today you will be with me in paradise."

What did Jesus do?
Do you believe anyone is too far gone to believe in Jesus? Why or why not?

Real-life response

Pray for a person you know who seems too far gone to want Jesus. Pray all day that God will give you a chance to say something to that person about your faith.

So how'd it go today?

1. Were you conscious of Jesus at all today? If so, when? If not, why not?

2. What, if anything, did you notice about yourself today?

3. What do you want to say to Jesus after today?
    Dear Jesus,

4. What would Jesus say to you after today?
    Dear _____,

Secret past

During the first couple of years after her dad left, Heather became sexually active with her boyfriend. After some counseling Heather realized that she was using sex as a way to drown her pain about her parents' divorce. She broke up with her boyfriend and, thanks to Karen, a church youth worker, Heather started taking her faith very seriously.

One night Heather's mother surprised her at the dinner table by asking her, "Have you been sexually active?"

Heather was so shocked at the directness of the question, she didn't know what to say. Her mother didn't know about Heather's past sexual activities, and Heather certainly didn't want to tell her now—especially since she had straightened out her life. Besides, her mother had enough to worry about without this new knowledge.

What do you think Jesus would do if he were Heather?

Not-so-secret past *Adapted from John 4*

So he came to a town in Samaria, and Jesus, tired as he was from the journey, sat down by the well.

When a Samaritan woman came to draw water, Jesus said to her, "Will you give me a drink?" (His disciples had gone into the town to buy food.)

The Samaritan woman said to him, "You are a Jew and I am a Samaritan woman. How can you ask me for a drink?" (For Jews do not associate with Samaritans.)

Jesus said, "Everyone who drinks this water will be thirsty again, but whoever drinks the water I give him will never thirst. Indeed, the water I give him will become in him a spring of water welling up to eternal life."

The woman said to him, "Sir, give me this water so that I won't get thirsty and have to keep coming here to draw water."

He told her, "Go, call your husband and come back."

"I have no husband," she replied.

Jesus said to her, "You are right when you say you have no husband. The fact is, you have had five husbands, and the man you now have is not your husband. What you have just said is quite true."

Then, leaving her water jar, the woman went back to the town and said to the people, "Come, see a man who told me everything I ever did. Could this be the Christ?" They came out of the town and made their way toward him.

Many of the Samaritans from that town believed in him because of the woman's testimony, "He told me everything I ever did."

What did Jesus do?
What would you have done if you were this woman? Would you have told everyone or been more discreet? Why?

Real-life response

Think of a way you can show kindness to one of your teachers today.

So how'd it go today?

1. Were you conscious of Jesus at all today? If so, when? If not, why not?

2. What, if anything, did you notice about yourself today?

3. What do you want to say to Jesus after today?
    Dear Jesus,

4. What would Jesus say to you after today?
    Dear _____,

Living in a perfect world

Spring Break Camp was awesome. God was so alive in everyone's life there. It was great to be at a place where there was no violence, no swearing, no fighting. Everyone was working together, helping each other, celebrating all the neat things happening in people's lives. I hadn't realized how negative school can be. All my friends are telling me to get out of the public school and go to a Christian school where everyone knows God and tries to act like a Christian. No gangs. No bad influences. How could God not want me to be where I can grow?

What would Jesus do?

Staying in a perfect world *Matthew 17:1-13*

After six days Jesus took with him Peter, James and John the brother of James, and led them up a high mountain by themselves. There he was transfigured before them. His face shone like the sun, and his clothes became as white as the light. Just then there appeared before them Moses and Elijah, talking with Jesus.

Peter said to Jesus, "Lord, it is good for us to be here. If you wish, I will put up three shelters—one for you, one for Moses and one for Elijah."

While he was still speaking, a bright cloud enveloped them, and a voice from the cloud said, "This is my Son, whom I love; with him I am well pleased. Listen to him!"

When the disciples heard this, they fell facedown to the ground, terrified. But Jesus came and touched them. "Get up," he said. "Don't be afraid." When they looked up, they saw no one except Jesus.

As they were coming down the mountain, Jesus instructed them, "Don't tell anyone what you have seen, until the Son of Man has been raised from the dead."

The disciples asked him, "Why then do the teachers of the law say that Elijah must come first?"

Jesus replied, "To be sure, Elijah comes and will restore all things. But I tell you, Elijah has already come, and they did not recognize him, but have done to him everything they wished. In the same way the Son of Man is going to suffer at their hands." Then the disciples understood that he was talking to them about John the Baptist.

What did Jesus do?

Verse 6 says the disciples were "terrified." Have you ever been terrified of God? Is being

terrified of God good, bad, or both?

Take 30 minutes today to be silent with God. Find a place that is quiet, where you cannot be interrupted, and ask God to be with you. If you want, journal quietly whatever thoughts come into your mind.

So how'd it go today?

1. Were you conscious of Jesus at all today? If so, when? If not, why not?

2. What, if anything, did you notice about yourself today?

3. What do you want to say to Jesus after today?
    Dear Jesus,

4. What would Jesus say to you after today?
    Dear _____,

day 15

Makin' the big bucks

I've got this school deal wired. My folks have been poor all their lives—but dude, I am not going for poverty. Going for the big coin, here. I am taking all college prep courses, studying every night until late, and working two jobs on the weekend. I'm looking forward to law degree and then . . . The Job. Sure, I won't forget where I came from. I'll share the wealth, but, baby, I ain't never going back to poverty.

What would Jesus say in response to this statement?

Hangin' on to the big bucks *Matthew 19:16-30*

Now a man came up to Jesus and asked, "Teacher, what good thing must I do to get eternal life?"

"Why do you ask me about what is good?" Jesus replied. "There is only One who is good. If you want to enter life, obey the commandments."

"Which ones?" the man inquired.

Jesus replied, " 'Do not murder, do not commit adultery, do not steal, do not give false testimony, honor your father and mother,' and 'love your neighbor as yourself.' "

"All these I have kept," the young man said. "What do I still lack?"

Jesus answered, "If you want to be perfect, go, sell your possessions and give to the poor, and you will have treasure in heaven. Then come, follow me."

When the young man heard this, he went away sad, because he had great wealth.

Then Jesus said to his disciples, "I tell you the truth, it is hard for a rich man to enter the kingdom of heaven. Again I tell you, it is easier for a camel to go through the eye of a needle than for a rich man to enter the kingdom of God."

When the disciples heard this, they were greatly astonished and asked, "Who then can be saved?"

Jesus looked at them and said, "With man this is impossible, but with God all things are possible."

Peter answered him, "We have left everything to follow you! What then will there be for us?"

Jesus said to them, "I tell you the truth, at the renewal of all things, when the Son of Man sits on his glorious throne, you who have followed me will also sit on 12 thrones, judging the 12 tribes of Israel. And everyone who has left houses or brothers or sisters or father or mother or children or fields for my sake will receive a hundred times as much and will inherit eternal life. But many who are first will be last, and many who are last will be first."

What did Jesus do with this man?

Where do you stand when it comes to money and Jesus? Do you believe you can be wealthy and still be a Christian? If so, why did Jesus let the rich young man go?

Real-life response

Find a project or charity to which you can give some money today.

So how'd it go today?

1. Were you conscious of Jesus at all today? If so, when? If not, why not?

2. What, if anything, did you notice about yourself today?

3. What do you want to say to Jesus after today?
    Dear Jesus,

4. What would Jesus say to you after today?
    Dear _____,

The middle of my 30-day adventure

Flip back and read your expectations you wrote for "The Beginning of My 30-Day Adventure." Go down the list and evaluate how you're doing. It is perfectly okay to cross out some of your expectations because they seem unreasonable or irrelevant now. Don't worry if you haven't met all of your expectations—or even come close. Just celebrate what you *have* done.

How am I doing now, considering the expectations I wrote down 15 days ago about—

My relationship with Jesus...

My parents...

My friends...

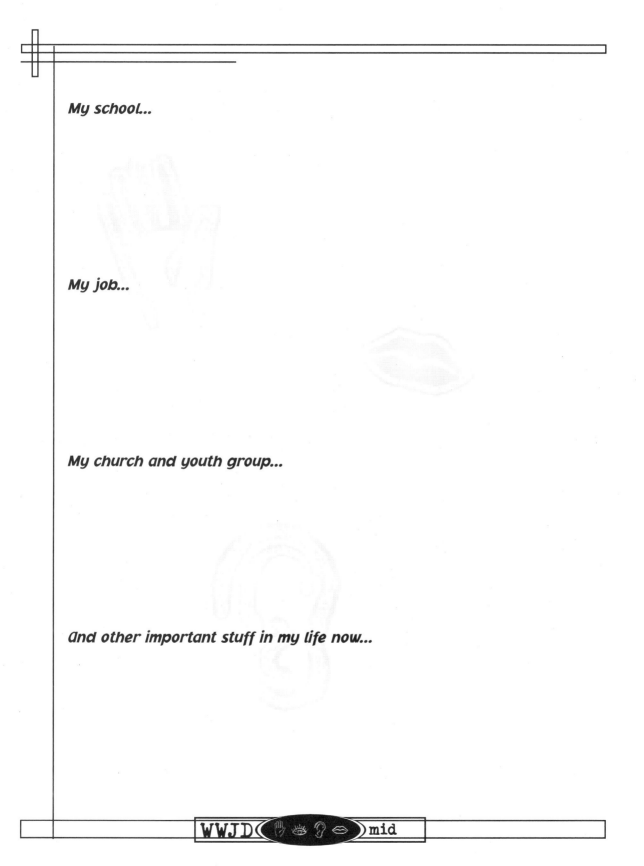

My school...

My job...

My church and youth group...

And other important stuff in my life now...

day 16

I'm a nobody

I'm going to be real honest with you. I'm a nobody. I don't even make a blip on the radar screen at school. I don't go out for any sports. I'm average looking. I don't really stand out with any talent. In fact, the only stand-out feature about me is my wheelchair.

The people who are nice to me are usually *too* nice, if you know what I mean. It's obvious they don't know me and they don't want to know me. To them I'm just a token disabled person. Don't get me wrong, though. There are plenty of kids who make fun of me. I'm used to that kind of treatment. It's just . . . well, like I said—I'm a nobody. Nobody cares. If I died tomorrow, besides my folks, who would really notice?

What would Jesus say to this person?

A bent-over somebody   *Luke 13:10-17*

On a Sabbath Jesus was teaching in one of the synagogues, and a woman was there who had been crippled by a spirit for 18 years. She was bent over and could not straighten up at all. When Jesus saw her, he called her forward and said to her, "Woman, you are set free from your infirmity." Then he put his hands on her, and immediately she straightened up and praised God.

Indignant because Jesus had healed on the Sabbath, the synagogue ruler said to the people, "There are six days for work. So come and be healed on those days, not on the Sabbath."

The Lord answered him, "You hypocrites! Doesn't each of you on the Sabbath untie his ox or donkey from the stall and lead it out to give it water? Then should not this woman, a daughter of Abraham, whom Satan has kept bound for 18 long years, be set free on the Sabbath day from what bound her?"

When he said this, all his opponents were humiliated, but the people were delighted with all the wonderful things he was doing.

What did Jesus do?
Jesus noticed the "nobody" and rebuked the "somebodies." What does that tell you about Jesus?

Real-life response

Think of someone at school who's flying below the popularity radar—someone who may consider herself to be a nobody. Do something today to make that person feel like a somebody.

So **how'd it** go today?

1. Were you conscious of Jesus at all today? If so, when? If not, why not?

2. What, if anything, did you notice about yourself today?

3. What do you want to say to Jesus after today?
   Dear Jesus,

4. What would Jesus say to you after today?
   Dear _____,

Obnoxious

Every day at school Sadie is in my face. She drives me crazy. Sure, she has lots of
friends—in fact, she has the best friends money can buy. She drives a new Mustang convertible (or should I say, a new *red* Mustang convertible). She's always flaunting her
money, her fancy clothes, and the fact that her father is some big-shot criminal attorney.
I'd like her to stay as far out of my life as possible. What a total jerk!

What would Jesus do around Sadie?

Ex-obnoxious *Luke 19:1-10*

Jesus entered Jericho and was passing through. A man was there by the name of
Zacchaeus; he was a chief tax collector and was wealthy. He wanted to see who Jesus
was, but being a short man he could not, because of the crowd. So he ran ahead and
climbed a sycamore-fig tree to see him, since Jesus was coming that way.

When Jesus reached the spot, he looked up and said to him, "Zacchaeus, come
down immediately. I must stay at your house today." So he came down at once and wel-
comed him gladly.

All the people saw this and began to mutter, "He has gone to be the guest of a
'sinner.' "

But Zacchaeus stood up and said to the Lord, "Look, Lord! Here and now I give
half of my possessions to the poor, and if I have cheated anybody out of anything, I will
pay back four times the amount."

Jesus said to him, "Today salvation has come to this house, because this man, too,
is a son of Abraham. For the Son of Man came to seek and to save what was lost."

What did Jesus do?

Many times in the Bible people were healed or changed by Jesus, and they were not
pleased. They were angry, afraid, or threatened, but they did not celebrate. Why? Why do
some people wish people would stay the same, even if the same is bad? Can you think of
some examples in your own life?

Real-life response

Think of someone you know who has changed for the better. Write or call that person to
affirm him.

1. Were you conscious of Jesus at all today? If so, when?
If not, why not?

2. What, if anything, did you notice about yourself today?

3. What do you want to say to Jesus after today?
       Dear Jesus,

4. What would Jesus say to you after today?
       Dear _____,

day 18

Did she or didn't she?

Sharon broke up with Ron last weekend because he was pushing her to have sex. The word around school is that Sharon is pregnant. But the fact is that Sharon *didn't* have sex with Ron because of her faith. Now she is devastated by the rumors. And she found out that Ron had apparently been telling all his friends that he and Sharon were having sex frequently. Sharon doesn't know what to do.

What do you think Jesus would tell Sharon to do?

Is he or isn't he? *Mark 15:1-5*

Very early in the morning, the chief priests, with the elders, the teachers of the law and the whole Sanhedrin, reached a decision. They bound Jesus, led him away and handed him over to Pilate.

"Are you the king of the Jews?" asked Pilate.

"Yes, it is as you say," Jesus replied.

The chief priests accused him of many things. So again Pilate asked him, "Aren't you going to answer? See how many things they are accusing you of."

But Jesus still made no reply, and Pilate was amazed.

What did Jesus do?
Why didn't Jesus speak up in verse 5?

Real-life response

Every time you see another student today, say a quick prayer for your school, something like "Jesus, please make yourself known at our school."

So how'd it go today?

1. Were you conscious of Jesus at all today? If so, when? If not, why not?

2. What, if anything, did you notice about yourself today?

3. What do you want to say to Jesus after today?
    Dear Jesus,

4. What would Jesus say to you after today?
    Dear _____,

Bad witness

A group of radical Christians on campus is causing a stir. They meet every morning for Bible study, they wear religious T-shirts, they constantly find ways to talk about Jesus in class, and they're always trying to witness to kids. I think it's great what these guys are doing, but it's just not me.

One of the leaders of the group, Rob, knows I'm a Christian and keeps hassling me to join the group. He keeps telling me I need to "get on fire for Jesus." He says I'm being a lukewarm Christian and I have to decide whether I'm going to follow Christ or not. He tells me I don't pray enough and I don't read my Bible enough. Lately he's been telling me he doesn't think I'm a Christian at all. I'm really confused. I live my Christian life differently from Rob and his group. I try to build relationships slowly with a couple of kids I know who aren't Christians—kids who are really turned off by Rob's group.

What would Jesus say to Rob?

Bad Sabbath-keeper *Matthew 12:1-13*

At that time Jesus went through the grainfields on the Sabbath. His disciples were hungry and began to pick some heads of grain and eat them. When the Pharisees saw this, they said to him, "Look! Your disciples are doing what is unlawful on the Sabbath."

He answered, "Haven't you read what David did when he and his companions were hungry? He entered the house of God, and he and his companions ate the consecrated bread—which was not lawful for them to do, but only for the priests. Or haven't you read in the Law that on the Sabbath the priests in the temple desecrate the day and yet are innocent? I tell you that one greater than the temple is here. If you had known what these words mean, 'I desire mercy, not sacrifice,' you would not have condemned the innocent. For the Son of Man is Lord of the Sabbath."

Going on from that place, he went into their synagogue, and a man with a shriveled hand was there. Looking for a reason to accuse Jesus, they asked him, "Is it lawful to heal on the Sabbath?"

He said to them, "If any of you has a sheep and it falls into a pit on the Sabbath, will you not take hold of it and lift it out? How much more valuable is a man than a sheep! Therefore it is lawful to do good on the Sabbath."

Then he said to the man, "Stretch out your hand." So he stretched it out and it was completely restored, just as sound as the other.

What did Jesus do?

Why did the Pharisees get so mad at Jesus and his disciples? Why are Christians so critical of other Christians? Would you consider Rob in the story above a Pharisee or just a concerned Christian?

Real-life response

Think of an adult in your church who you really appreciate. Call or write that person and tell him why you appreciate him.

So how'd it go today?

1. Were you conscious of Jesus at all today? If so, when? If not, why not?

2. What, if anything, did you notice about yourself today?

3. What do you want to say to Jesus after today?
   Dear Jesus,

4. What would Jesus say to you after today?
   Dear _____ ,

Where's God?

People at church are always talking about the presence of God in their lives. Some say they can hear God speak to them. Others say they just know when God is present. I read the Bible and I pray all the time, but I can honestly say I've never really experienced God. Does that mean I'm not a Christian? Does it mean I'm not trying hard enough? I'm really confused—and a little scared, too. I really want to experience God in my life.

What would Jesus say?

Where's Jesus? *Luke 24:13-35*

Now that same day two of them were going to a village called Emmaus, about seven miles from Jerusalem. They were talking with each other about everything that had happened. As they talked and discussed these things with each other, Jesus himself came up and walked along with them; but they were kept from recognizing him.

He asked them, "What are you discussing together as you walk along?"

They stood still, their faces downcast. One of them, named Cleopas, asked him, "Are you only a visitor to Jerusalem and do not know the things that have happened there in these days?"

"What things?" he asked.

About Jesus of Nazareth," they replied. "He was a prophet, powerful in word and deed before God and all the people. The chief priests and our rulers handed him over to be sentenced to death, and they crucified him; but we had hoped that he was the one who was going to redeem Israel. And what is more, it is the third day since all this took place. In addition, some of our women amazed us. They went to the tomb early this morning but didn't find his body. They came and told us that they had seen a vision of angels, who said he was alive. Then some of our companions went to the tomb and found it just as the women had said, but him they did not see."

He said to them, "How foolish you are, and how slow of heart to believe all that the prophets have spoken! Did not the Christ have to suffer these things and then enter his glory?" And beginning with Moses and all the Prophets, he explained to them what was said in all the Scriptures concerning himself.

As they approached the village to which they were going, Jesus acted as if he were going farther. But they urged him strongly, "Stay with us, for it is nearly evening; the day is almost over." So he went in to stay with them.

When he was at the table with them, he took bread, gave thanks, broke it and began to give it to them. Then their eyes were opened and they recognized him, and he disappeared from their sight. They asked each other, "Were not our hearts burning within us while he talked with us on the road and opened the Scriptures to us?"

They got up and returned at once to Jerusalem. There they found the Eleven and those with them, assembled together and saying, "It is true! The Lord has risen and has appeared to Simon." Then the two told what had happened on the way, and how Jesus was recognized by them when he broke the bread.

What did Jesus do to make himself known to these men?

Have you ever experienced God? If so, when? If not, why not call your youth worker and talk to him about how that can happen?

Real-life response

Before school today, ask the Lord to make himself known to you in a special way. Then keep your eyes, ears, and heart open so that you may experience God's presence.

So how'd it go today?

**1. Were you conscious of Jesus at all today? If so, when?
If not, why not?**

2. What, if anything, did you notice about yourself today?

3. What do you want to say to Jesus after today?
   Dear Jesus,

4. What would Jesus say to you after today?
   Dear _____ ,

day 21

Who do I serve?

I've been on service projects before. They're cool. I've built houses for the poor, worked in an inner-city preschool, and repainted houses in the Appalachians. I like doing things for others. But when I get home, back into my neighborhood and my school, I don't know now to serve. I mean, what do I do, go up to a kid at school and offer him some money?

What would Jesus do?

Who is my neighbor? *Luke 10:25-37*

On one occasion an expert in the law stood up to test Jesus. "Teacher," he asked, "what must I do to inherit eternal life?"

"What is written in the Law?" he replied. "How do you read it?"

He answered: " 'Love the Lord your God with all your heart and with all your soul and with all your strength and with all your mind'; and, 'Love your neighbor as yourself.' "

"You have answered correctly," Jesus replied. "Do this and you will live."

But he wanted to justify himself, so he asked Jesus, "And who is my neighbor?"

In reply Jesus said: "A man was going down from Jerusalem to Jericho, when he fell into the hands of robbers. They stripped him of his clothes, beat him and went away, leaving him half dead. A priest happened to be going down the same road, and when he saw the man, he passed by on the other side. So too, a Levite, when he came to the place and saw him, passed by on the other side. But a Samaritan, as he traveled, came where the man was; and when he saw him, he took pity on him. He went to him and bandaged his wounds, pouring on oil and wine. Then he put the man on his own donkey, took him to an inn and took care of him. The next day he took out two silver coins and gave them to the innkeeper. 'Look after him,' he said, 'and when I return, I will reimburse you for any extra expense you may have.'

"Which of these three do you think was a neighbor to the man who fell into the hands of robbers?"

The expert in the law replied, "The one who had mercy on him."

Jesus told him, "Go and do likewise."

What did Jesus say?
List some ways you could serve your "neighbor."

Real-life response

Secretly serve someone in your neighborhood. Wash a car, mow a lawn, rake leaves, or do something else without letting the person know who did it.

So how'd it go today?

1. Were you conscious of Jesus at all today? If so, when? If not, why not?

2. What, if anything, did you notice about yourself today?

3. What do you want to say to Jesus after today?
    Dear Jesus,

4. What would Jesus say to you after today?
    Dear _____ ,

day 22

The most important thing

The most important thing any Christian can do is tell others about Jesus. Think about it. Without Jesus people don't have life, they don't have forgiveness, they don't have joy. Without Jesus they don't have much to look forward to. I figure I can't waste time helping people, hoping they will see Jesus. Not me. I'm telling everyone I see about Jesus. My job is to win as many kids to Christ as I can, and that's what I'm doing.

What would Jesus say to this person?

Well, maybe this is the most important thing _John 13:1-17_

It was just before the Passover Feast. Jesus knew that the time had come for him to leave this world and go to the Father. Having loved his own who were in the world, he now showed them the full extent of his love.

The evening meal was being served, and the devil had already prompted Judas Iscariot, son of Simon, to betray Jesus. Jesus knew that the Father had put all things under his power, and that he had come from God and was returning to God; so he got up from the meal, took off his outer clothing, and wrapped a towel around his waist. After that, he poured water into a basin and began to wash his disciples' feet, drying them with the towel that was wrapped around him.

He came to Simon Peter, who said to him, "Lord, are you going to wash my feet?"

Jesus replied, "You do not realize now what I am doing, but later you will understand."

"No," said Peter, "you shall never wash my feet."

Jesus answered, "Unless I wash you, you have no part with me."

"Then, Lord," Simon Peter replied, "not just my feet but my hands and my head as well!"

Jesus answered, "A person who has had a bath needs only to wash his feet; his whole body is clean. And you are clean, though not every one of you." For he knew who was going to betray him, and that was why he said not every one was clean.

When he had finished washing their feet, he put on his clothes and returned to his place. "Do you understand what I have done for you?" he asked them. "You call me 'Teacher' and 'Lord,' and rightly so, for that is what I am. Now that I, your Lord and Teacher, have washed your feet, you also should wash one another's feet. I have set you an example that you should do as I have done for you. I tell you the truth, no servant is greater than his master, nor is a messenger greater than the one who sent him. Now that you know these things, you will be blessed if you do them."

What did Jesus do?
What is the most important witness for Christians?

Real-life response

Give each member of your family a "coupon" good for things like washing the dishes when it's not your turn, vacuuming the house, turning off your stereo when you're asked to, and not using the phone for a whole day.

So how'd it go today?

1. Were you conscious of Jesus at all today? If so, when? If not, why not?

2. What, if anything, did you notice about yourself today?

3. What do you want to say to Jesus after today?
    Dear Jesus,

4. What would Jesus say to you after today?
    Dear _____,

How do I say it?

I was sitting by myself at lunch trying to cram for my history test when another band member, Laurie, sat down next to me. Although we're friends in band, we hardly ever talk. I certainly didn't want to talk to her during my cram session. I was as nice as I could be, but I kept on studying, hoping Laurie wouldn't stay long. After a minute or so, I realized she wasn't leaving.

I turned to talk to her and noticed she was crying. "What's the matter, Laurie?" I asked.

She looked me square in the eye and asked, "How do you become a Christian?"

You could have knocked me over with a feather. "Are you serious?" I stumbled.

"I'm dead serious, Carolyn. My life's a disaster right now with my folks in the middle of a divorce. I know you go to church. I saw you at the See You at the Pole day praying for all of us. So, tell me, how do I get what you have?"

Man, talk about shock. I tried to tell her the best I could. I didn't have my Bible with me, so I think I butchered a bunch of Scriptures. I know I didn't make any sense. But I asked her if she wanted to pray and ask Jesus into her life and she said yes! I couldn't believe it. That was last night. Now what?

What would Jesus do?

How do I do it? *John 3:1-16*

Now there was a man of the Pharisees named Nicodemus, a member of the Jewish ruling council. He came to Jesus at night and said, "Rabbi, we know you are a teacher who has come from God. For no one could perform the miraculous signs you are doing if God were not with him."

In reply Jesus declared, "I tell you the truth, no one can see the kingdom of God unless he is born again."

"How can a man be born when he is old?" Nicodemus asked. "Surely he cannot enter a second time into his mother's womb to be born!"

Jesus answered, "I tell you the truth, no one can enter the kingdom of God unless he is born of water and the Spirit. Flesh gives birth to flesh, but the Spirit gives birth to spirit. You should not be surprised at my saying, 'You must be born again.' The wind blows wherever it pleases. You hear its sound, but you cannot tell where it comes from or where it is going. So it is with everyone born of the Spirit."

"How can this be?" Nicodemus asked.

"You are Israel's teacher," said Jesus, "and do you not understand these things? I tell you the truth, we speak of what we know, and we testify to what we have seen, but still you people do not accept our testimony. I have spoken to you of earthly things and you do not believe; how then will you believe if I speak of heavenly things? No one has ever gone into heaven except the one who came from heaven—the Son of Man. Just as Moses lifted up the snake in the desert, so the Son of Man must be lifted up, that everyone who believes in him may have eternal life.

"For God so loved the world that he gave his one and only Son, that whoever believes in him shall not perish but have eternal life."

What did Jesus do?
What's the best way to help a new Christian?

Real-life response

Volunteer one Sunday a month to help kids younger than you learn about Jesus.

So how'd it go today?

1. Were you conscious of Jesus at all today? If so, when? If not, why not?

2. What, if anything, did you notice about yourself today?

3. What do you want to say to Jesus after today?
Dear Jesus,

4. What would Jesus say to you after today?
Dear _____,

day 24

Doubting Diane

Okay, I have lots and lots of questions. I drive my teachers crazy. I drive my parents crazy. I drive myself crazy. But I can't help it—questions just pop into my head. I try to stop them, but they don't stop.

I am a Christian. At least, I *think* I'm a Christian. See, there I go. I doubt that I'm a Christian half the time and doubt that Christianity is true the rest of the time. If Jesus were sitting here right now, would I have a ton of questions for him! But I wonder if he'd answer them, or send a bolt of lightning to zap me.

What would Jesus say to this person?

Doubting Thomas   *John 20:19-31*

On the evening of that first day of the week, when the disciples were together, with the doors locked for fear of the Jews, Jesus came and stood among them and said, "Peace be with you!" After he said this, he showed them his hands and side. The disciples were overjoyed when they saw the Lord.

Again Jesus said, "Peace be with you! As the Father has sent me, I am sending you." And with that he breathed on them and said, "Receive the Holy Spirit. If you forgive anyone his sins, they are forgiven; if you do not forgive them, they are not forgiven."

Now Thomas (called Didymus), one of the Twelve, was not with the disciples when Jesus came. So the other disciples told him, "We have seen the Lord!"

But he said to them, "Unless I see the nail marks in his hands and put my finger where the nails were, and put my hand into his side, I will not believe it."

A week later his disciples were in the house again, and Thomas was with them. Though the doors were locked, Jesus came and stood among them and said, "Peace be with you!" Then he said to Thomas, "Put your finger here; see my hands. Reach out your hand and put it into my side. Stop doubting and believe."

Thomas said to him, "My Lord and my God!"

Then Jesus told him, "Because you have seen me, you have believed; blessed are those who have not seen and yet have believed."

Jesus did many other miraculous signs in the presence of his disciples, which are not recorded in this book. But these are written that you may believe that Jesus is the Christ, the Son of God, and that by believing you may have life in his name.

What did Jesus do?

Do you think doubts are healthy or unhealthy? Why?

Real-life response

Think of one area of your life in which you need Jesus' help. Pray for his help at the beginning of each hour today.

So how'd it go today?

1. Were you conscious of Jesus at all today? If so, when? If not, why not?

2. What, if anything, did you notice about yourself today?

3. What do you want to say to Jesus after today?
   Dear Jesus,

4. What would Jesus say to you after today?
   Dear _____,

day 25

Smothered

I know I'm supposed to do all this stuff for Jesus, but sometimes I wonder if Jesus ever thinks about *us.* Does he know that life is stressful—even when you're 16? I'm overwhelmed with school, sports, work, parents, and church. I feel like I'm being smothered by everything I have to do. Does Jesus understand? Is he sympathetic or would he lecture me on using my time better?

What would Jesus say?

Blinded *Luke 18:35-43*

As Jesus approached Jericho, a blind man was sitting by the roadside begging. When he heard the crowd going by, he asked what was happening. They told him, "Jesus of Nazareth is passing by."

He called out, "Jesus, Son of David, have mercy on me!"

Those who led the way rebuked him and told him to be quiet, but he shouted all the more, "Son of David, have mercy on me!"

Jesus stopped and ordered the man to be brought to him. When he came near, Jesus asked him, "What do you want me to do for you?"

"Lord, I want to see," he replied.

Jesus said to him, "Receive your sight; your faith has healed you." Immediately he received his sight and followed Jesus, praising God. When all the people saw it, they also praised God.

What did Jesus do?
Are you afraid of Jesus or are you willing to ask for help no matter what?

Real-life response

Think of someone you know who needs help. Offer to help that person, then follow through on your offer.

1. Were you conscious of Jesus at all today? If so, when? If not, why not?

2. What, if anything, did you notice about yourself today?

3. What do you want to say to Jesus after today?
     Dear Jesus,

4. What would Jesus say to you after today?
     Dear _____,

day 26

Wild man

My friends and I are a little crazy. We like to have a good time, so we're always messing around. People look at us like we're nuts. That's okay. We don't mind if people think we're crazy. Unfortunately, though, most people get mad at us—even at church. The youth minister is always telling us to grow up, to act more mature, to get serious. I *am* serious, serious about not being serious. Most people are too serious. Seems like they never laugh.

Tonight was the low point. After youth group, a bunch of kids and sponsors sat down with us and told us we either needed to get serious or get out of the group. We don't disrupt the meetings, we liven them up. I don't get it.

What would Jesus say?

Drunk man *Matthew 11:19*

"The Son of Man came eating and drinking, and they say, 'Here is a glutton and a drunkard, a friend of tax collectors and "sinners." ' But wisdom is proved right by her actions."

Wild children *Matthew 19:13-15*

Then little children were brought to Jesus for him to place his hands on them and pray for them. But the disciples rebuked those who brought them.

Jesus said, "Let the little children come to me, and do not hinder them, for the kingdom of heaven belongs to such as these." When he had placed his hands on them, he went on from there.

What did people say about Jesus?
What did you learn about Jesus in these two incidents?

Real-life response

Suggest to your family that you play a game together. (Hide and Seek is a great family game.)

1. *Were you conscious of Jesus at all today? If so, when?*
If not, why not?

2. *What, if anything, did you notice about yourself today?*

3. *What do you want to say to Jesus after today?*
     Dear Jesus,

4. *What would Jesus say to you after today?*
     Dear _____,

Bad year

What a year. My relationship with Jesus has been a disaster—just like my home life. My folks fight all the time. My brother's gone the heavy-metal-punker route, my sister's in and out of trouble, and I'm just trying to keep my head above water. I'm trying to hang on, but sometimes I wonder what happened to Jesus. Does he ever show up when you're not in a good place?

What would Jesus do?

Bad storm   *Mark 4:35-41*

That day when evening came, he said to his disciples, "Let us go over to the other side." Leaving the crowd behind, they took him along, just as he was, in the boat. There were also other boats with him. A furious squall came up, and the waves broke over the boat, so that it was nearly swamped. Jesus was in the stern, sleeping on a cushion. The disciples woke him and said to him, "Teacher, don't you care if we drown?"

He got up, rebuked the wind and said to the waves, "Quiet! Be still!" Then the wind died down and it was completely calm.

He said to his disciples, "Why are you so afraid? Do you still have no faith?"

They were terrified and asked each other, "Who is this? Even the wind and the waves obey him!"

What did Jesus do?
Someone has said that waiting is not doing nothing, it's doing something. Do you find it hard to wait for Jesus to show up?

Real-life response

See if you can spot Jesus today. When the day is over, see if you can recall any moments when you were conscious of Jesus' presence.

So **how'd it** go today?

**1. Were you conscious of Jesus at all today? If so, when?
If not, why not?**

2. What, if anything, did you notice about yourself today?

3. What do you want to say to Jesus after today?
    Dear Jesus,

4. What would Jesus say to you after today?
    Dear _____,

Is it okay to cry?

I'm 18 and the captain and 240-pound center of one of our state's top football teams. My nickname is Animal. I come from a pretty tough family. Both my parents were alcoholics and our home was hell. I was drinking every weekend, barely getting through school. Then our neighbor dragged my dad to some men's deal called Promise Keepers. My dad meets Jesus, comes home sober, takes my mom and me to church, and we both accept Jesus. Talk about night and day. Our family has been a miracle since then. I can't get over it. My mom stopped drinking. I stopped drinking. My grades improved.

This is the weird part: every time I think about our family, I start crying. It's not like I'm wailing or anything, but my eyes fill up with tears. I'm sort of embarrassed about it, and yet I'm not. I mean, I'm so grateful. I know some people think it's uncool for a guy like me—for Animal—to cry. All the guys in my church tell me I need to get a grip and quit crying at every youth group meeting.

What would Jesus say?

Is it okay to waste perfume? *Luke 7:36-50*

Now one of the Pharisees invited Jesus to have dinner with him, so he went to the Pharisee's house and reclined at the table. When a woman who had lived a sinful life in that town learned that Jesus was eating at the Pharisee's house, she brought an alabaster jar of perfume, and as she stood behind him at his feet weeping, she began to wet his feet with her tears. Then she wiped them with her hair, kissed them and poured perfume on them.

When the Pharisee who had invited him saw this, he said to himself, "If this man were a prophet, he would know who is touching him and what kind of woman she is— that she is a sinner."

Jesus answered him, "Simon, I have something to tell you."

"Tell me, teacher," he said.

"Two men owed money to a certain moneylender. One owed him 500 denarii, and the other 50. Neither of them had the money to pay him back, so he canceled the debts of both. Now which of them will love him more?"

Simon replied, "I suppose the one who had the bigger debt canceled."

"You have judged correctly," Jesus said.

Then he turned toward the woman and said to Simon, "Do you see this woman? I came into your house. You did not give me any water for my feet, but she wet my feet with her tears and wiped them with her hair. You did not give me a kiss, but this woman, from the time I entered, has not stopped kissing my feet. You did not put oil on my head, but she has poured perfume on my feet. Therefore, I tell you, her many sins have been forgiven—for she loved much. But he who has been forgiven little loves little."

Then Jesus said to her, "Your sins are forgiven."

What did Jesus do?
Why is gratitude so difficult?

Real-life response

List all the things in your life that you're grateful for. Spend the day saying, "Thank you, Jesus" every time you think of something you're grateful for.

So how'd it go today?

1. Were you conscious of Jesus at all today? If so, when? If not, why not?

2. What, if anything, did you notice about yourself today?

3. What do you want to say to Jesus after today?
Dear Jesus,

4. What would Jesus say to you after today?
Dear _____,

When?

My dad has Lou Gehrig's disease. It has to be one of the most terrible diseases there is. Watching my father wither up and die is killing our whole family. I know there is a God and I know he loves us—but why does he allow diseases like this? I'm trying to understand. I'm trying to be strong for my father and my mother, but my faith is starting to buckle under the strain. When is all this pain and suffering going to stop? My friends try to explain to me why we have sickness and dying. They show me Scriptures and pray with me. I appreciate all they're doing, but I wonder what would happen if Jesus showed up.

Where is Jesus?

Hurry   *Revelation 21:1-7*

Then I saw a new heaven and a new earth, for the first heaven and the first earth had passed away, and there was no longer any sea. I saw the Holy City, the new Jerusalem, coming down out of heaven from God, prepared as a bride beautifully dressed for her husband. And I heard a loud voice from the throne saying, "Now the dwelling of God is with men, and he will live with them. They will be his people, and God himself will be with them and be their God. He will wipe every tear from their eyes. There will be no more death or mourning or crying or pain, for the old order of things has passed away."

He who was seated on the throne said, "I am making everything new!" Then he said, "Write this down, for these words are trustworthy and true."

He said to me: "It is done. I am the Alpha and the Omega, the Beginning and the End. To him who is thirsty I will give to drink without cost from the spring of the water of life. He who overcomes will inherit all this, and I will be his God and he will be my son."

What is Jesus going to do?

Christians believe that someday there will be no more pain and suffering, but what about now? Does Jesus show up even in our pain and suffering?

Write a quick answer to the question "Why does God allow suffering?"

So how'd it go today?

1. Were you conscious of Jesus at all today? If so, when?
If not, why not?

2. What, if anything, did you notice about yourself today?

3. What do you want to say to Jesus after today?
Dear Jesus,

4. What would Jesus say to you after today?
Dear _____,

day 30

Life is hard, but it's good

This Christian life is hard. Every day brings new opportunities to deny my faith. It takes so much faith to survive now. Drugs, alcohol, sex—they're easy to find, too easy to get. It's hard to focus on God while your friends seem to be having a better time than you are. I try to convince my friends that life isn't as it appears and that someday they will regret the decisions they're making now. They just laugh. It sure seems lonely out here in the real world. How do I keep trying?

What would Jesus say?

Rowing is hard, but it's worth it *Matthew 14:22-32*

Immediately Jesus made the disciples get into the boat and go on ahead of him to the other side, while he dismissed the crowd. After he had dismissed them, he went up on a mountainside by himself to pray. When evening came, he was there alone, but the boat was already a considerable distance from land, buffeted by the waves because the wind was against it.

During the fourth watch of the night Jesus went out to them, walking on the lake. When the disciples saw him walking on the lake, they were terrified. "It's a ghost," they said, and cried out in fear.

But Jesus immediately said to them: "Take courage! It is I. Don't be afraid."

"Lord, if it's you," Peter replied, "tell me to come to you on the water."

"Come," he said.

Then Peter got down out of the boat, walked on the water and came toward Jesus. But when he saw the wind, he was afraid and, beginning to sink, cried out, "Lord, save me!"

Immediately Jesus reached out his hand and caught him. "You of little faith," he said, "why did you doubt?"

And when they climbed into the boat, the wind died down.

What did Jesus do for the disciples?

Dear Jesus, this is the last day of my 30-day adventure with you. Reading about you every day has brought me closer to you. I have always known we are supposed to read the Bible, but these last twenty-nine days haven't felt like supposed-to, they have felt like want-to. It's been want-to because of you. I had no idea you are so fascinating, so excit-

ing, so real. I didn't know a person like me could feel close to you. Thank you.

Real-life response

Write your own thank you to Jesus for the past 30 days.

So how'd it go today?

1. Were you conscious of Jesus at all today? If so, when? If not, why not?

2. What, if anything, did you notice about yourself today?

3. What do you want to say to Jesus after today?
Dear Jesus,

4. What would Jesus say to you after today?
Dear _____,

The end of my 30-day adventure

Write a letter to Jesus explaining in detail what has happened to you in the past 30 days. This is more than a thank-you letter—it's a letter to your friend, Jesus, telling him everything that went on in the last month.

Dear Jesus,
It's been quite a month...